Who'd think in Elementary

I'd see the Penitentiary

A Memoir of Brent Jackson

Copyright © 2014, 2020 by **Brent Jackson**

The scanning, uploading, and distribution of this book without permission is a theft of the author's intellectual property. If you would like permission to use material from the book (other than for review purposes), please contact dymondsentiments@gmail.com

Thank you for your support of the author's rights.

ISBN: 978-0-578-86601-7

Cover design: DH Art & Design LLC

Editor: Janine Folks

TABLE OF CONTENTS

Dedication 4

Acknowledgements 5

FOREWORD 8

1: IN THE BEGINNING 11

2: THE BREAKDOWN 15

3: SCHOOL DAYS 25

4: SISTER LOVE 31

5: DEAR DAD 35

6: TEMPTATION 39

7: LOVE ARRIVES 47

8: BAD DECISION 53

9: FINDING FREEDOM 63

10: RELEASED 69

11: RECOVERY 83

12: DYMOND LIFE 93

BIO OF BRENT JACKSON 98

DEDICATION

I dedicate this book to the memory of my Dad, the late Richard Jerome Jackson. To my Mom Mrs. Jo Ann who taught me how to love people unconditionally by loving me when I felt like I was unlovable.

To Larry & Red my Father-in-law and Mother-in-law who has always treated me like one of their own. To my son Tez whom I love dearly for allowing me to enter into his life and become a father figure to him when he was only 8 years old.

Last but not least, to my Beautiful Queen Chantelle who has loved me unconditionally even when I didn't have it all together. Thank you for keeping a fire underneath me and pushing me during the times when I grew weary. I trust that those arguments over the years were not in vain.

All Glory To God.

ACKNOWLEDGEMENTS

Deacon Brent Jackson is a faithful man of God who shares his remarkable life story in his book, **Who'd Think in Elementary, I'd see the Penitentiary?** It's an all too familiar tale of someone who experienced childhood trauma which led to a life of bad decisions, crime, and punishment as a young adult.

But, unique in this story is the underlying hope that eventually brings the man from the mess. By God's grace and Brent Jackson's tenacity, he has emerged as a man of faith and dedication who we are honored to serve with every week.

Sheryl Brady, Pastor

The Potter's House of North Dallas Frisco, TX

Brent Jackson's Memoir, **Who'd Think in Elementary I'd See the Penitentiary**... took me on a journey of amazing survival in unimaginable circumstances. This enthralling account took me to a place I could not go otherwise and it made me feel like I was right there with him experiencing the good, the bad, the hopefulness, the despair, the desperation and redemption of his life.

This compelling story is evidence that the human spirit is resilient, love changes things and with God, all things are possible. This book helped me to tap into my empathy to relate to a person I might have otherwise judged too harshly. This is a captivating easy to read narrative that everyone should experience.

I am so grateful that the story is being told and it will humanize those who find themselves in the penal system. This story was screaming to be told and I commend Mr. Jackson for his transparency in sharing his life story. I thank God for this powerful testimony of transformation. It is a reminder of God's grace and the power of **LOVE**.

~ Janine Folks, *Get the Pen*

I would also like to acknowledge the following individuals who have contributed to the publication of this book.

- Lovie Hooks (Step Mom)
- Uncle Melvan Johnson
- Adrian Simpson
- Valerie Lockett
- Kimika Chappell
- Rod Chappell
- Christine & Mark Morgan
- Carlos Young
- Janine Folks
- Setra Macala – You're Worth It Magazine
- Sam Palmore
- Deacon JD Lee
- The Potter's House Deacons Ministry
- The Potter's House Prison Ministry
- National Men's Prayer Call
- John L Mack – GPS: Get Published Successfully

FOREWORD

I met Brent Jackson over 20 years ago, inside the penitentiary, when he joined the Chance For Life Program (CFL). CFL is a transformational program based on Biblical principles. By the end of the first class, I knew that Brent was a young man with potential and with some guidance, one day he would do something great. He had a passion for learning and he followed all the rules, which led me to believe that he would not be coming back to prison as many others do.

After Brent was released from prison, he went through some challenges but was smart enough to reach out to those the Lord had put in his life. He would call whenever he needed someone to talk to. It was during this period in his life, I witnessed him getting closer and closer to God. Brent has transformed himself and what you might not see in him is the tremendous love for the

Lord that he exhibits in his life. His desire to help others by giving back is a testimony of the man he has become. When he was confronted with the question, "are you ready to change"? He was ready and he did change.

In reading the **book "Who'd Think in Elementary I'd see the Penitentiary",** I saw a young boy whose life was similar to many other young boys that face the struggles of the street and a school system that often fail to reach them. I also saw a family structure that did not give him the proper tools to navigate through life. I saw a young person that didn't have any hope of beating the prison system. From Detroit to Tennessee to Dallas, Brent Jackson has proven it's not how bad your circumstances are but how you respond to those circumstances.

Brent had dreams; dreams of working in the entertainment industry, dreams of family and dreams of doing the right thing is what kept him focused when he found himself in difficult places.

While written primarily to help young people, this book is essential reading for anyone who wants to increase their ability to make good decisions. It will guide you through everyday choices and experiences and give you the skills necessary to become responsible adults. If you need to find the courage, strength and confidence to stay the course, I strongly recommend to everyone to read this book and share it with the young people in your life.

Thomas J. Adams

President

Chance For Life Organization

Detroit, MI

1: IN THE BEGINNING

I JoAnn Jackson at Crittenton Hospital on was born on Nov. 5 1968 to Richard and Woodrow Wilson, close to Webb on the Westside of Detroit. We started out living at 1404 Pingree right off of Byron and then not too long after, moved to 9117 Appoline close to Joy Rd.

We were still in Detroit, Michigan. We later moved from Appoline and Joy Rd. to 19130 Woodingham right off of 7 mile, still in Detroit. We lived directly across the street from the Multi Grammy Award winning Gospel group, the Winans. I remember watching their family pile up in a station wagon headed to church back in the early 70's on several occasions before they became famous.

I attended Pasteur Elementary School while living on Woodingham Street. Still to this day, I can remember my kindergarten teacher's name. It was Ms. Lemon. I don't remember much about Ms. Lemon other than her name and that she was very nice to me. Her name will reside in my memory for the rest of my days.

One of the memories that I have while attending Pasteur Elementary was the time I left school (kindergarten) after we were dismissed to go home. I was supposed to wait in front of the school for my Mom to pick me up but I decided to go to the store instead. I wanted to buy some bubble gum that came with funny character trading cards inside. To make it even worst, the store that I walked to was across a big street in Detroit named

Livernois Avenue. I did not cross at the traffic light either. While I was shopping for bubble gum, my mom was at my school completely hysterical because she couldn't find me. After purchasing my bubble gum I decided that I was going to walk home (which was several blocks away) so I could prove to everyone that I was a big boy and I knew how to get home by myself.

After my mom circled a few blocks searching for me, she finally noticed me crossing Outer Drive street headed home. She whipped up on me like she was the police trying to apprehend a suspect. She told me to get my ass in the car and asked me what I was thinking. She remained silent the rest of the way home with her jaws tight. At this point I knew that once we arrived home and walked through that front door I was about to experience a whipping that I had never experienced before in my life.

Mama told me to go upstairs, take off my clothes and to wait on her. I was terrified of what was to come, but after several taps with a lightweight yard stick that didn't really hurt, I knew then that my mama was really trying to hurt me. My feelings were hurt more than anything so I cried until I eventually went to sleep.

Now I'm not really sure about what happened between my mom and dad but what I can recall is that all hell rang out between them which led to a very violent and nasty divorce. It was because of their divorce that we eventually lost our home.

During this time I was shuffled around a bit to get me away from the drama. I remember spending time with my sister and brother at their dad's house. I affectionately called him Bubba, but I also considered him to be my stepdad because he cared for me as if I was one of his son's. Bubba lived on a street named Kentucky, which was right off of Puritan Ave.

Eventually, I was sent to my maternal Grandmother's house

(my mom's mom) on Lee Place, which was right off of Byron in Detroit.

It was at this house where I witnessed my dad get shot by my mom for trying to jump on her because she wanted a divorce. It was Easter time because I remember eating a lot of jelly beans and my dad stopping me in my tracks saying to me "Stop eating all those jelly beans and go upstairs!" I heard the front door opening once I got close to the top of the landing. It was my mom and my Aunt Beverly coming in. I was playing with some Play-Doh in one of the rooms upstairs but once I started hearing a commotion downstairs I proceeded to go closer to see what was going on.

I was in the middle of the stairwell when I heard running, a loud crash of furniture hit the floor along with a loud Boom followed by seeing my dad laying on the floor by the front door saying "JoAnn don't leave, JoAnn don't leave me." To witness this with my own eyes was very traumatic but this was only the beginning of the journey God had already pre-ordained for me to travel.

2: THE BREAKDOWN

My result of all that had happened leading why mom had a nervous breakdown as a up to the divorce. Having to defend herself from getting hurt by my dad took a toll on her. I am so very grateful to God that my dad survived the shooting because he was a great dad who loved me more than any words could convey.

After my dad survived the shooting and healed up a bit, he returned to our home on Woodingham one evening with his rifle. One of our family friends that was also our neighbor across the street told us that after he had banged on the doors and windows for a while with his rifle in hand, he stood up on top of his car with his rifle and shot up the house. I'm not sure what would've happened if we were at home, but I thank God today that we will never really know for sure either will we. I remember that night vividly.

We pulled up in my Mama's blue 4 door 1969 Oldsmobile 98 and I was in the backseat singing along to one of my favorite songs back then on the radio "Bennie And The Jets" by Elton John. We went to check on the house that evening but the electricity had been turned off and it was super dark inside. After realizing that my Dad had been there and had shot up the house, I remember feeling afraid at the thought that I could possibly witness again what I had recently witnessed at my Grandmother's house.

While all of this divorce stuff was going on with my mom and pops, I was separated from my mom for a while and sent to one of my Aunts for the weekend to play with my cousins, or I was sent to stay longer at times during the summer vacation months. I'm not sure who took me that day but I remember visiting my mom one day while she was living at my aunt Ernestine's house on Freeland off of Fenkell Ave on the west side of Detroit. Mama was living in Aunt Ernie's basement and had started dating some new dude named Reggie who was a painter and seemed to know his craft really well. He had done some contract work for my Aunt Loretta on some of the real estate she prepped for sale. He had also painted and laid wallpaper at my Aunt Bev and Uncle Philips house back then off of 8mile and it looked really good to. Wall Paper was definitely in back then. During that time

I didn't care a whole lot about who my Mom was with, I just wanted her to take me along with her too. Don't get me wrong though, I was also concerned about her looking happier and functioning in a better mood than she had previously done in the past. Reggie was helping her feel better it seemed and I was okay with that. During this time my mom was pretty vulnerable. She fell for his smooth charm and began a committed relationship with him with no idea what was in store for her after deciding to say "I do" at the altar. I have to admit that Reggie was fun in the beginning.

He used to play this game where you had to

connect forehead to forehead and stare into each other's eyes and make faces until someone laughed. The person who laughed lost. I lost every time because I was full of smiles all the time anyway. I couldn't help it, I loved to smile back then. Reggie had a perm and wore his hair slick back like Superfly. He was also a member of a corvette stingray club until he totaled his corvette after entering the expressway at a very high speed, losing control and almost killing himself. He said he walked away without a scratch.

During the beginning of Mama and Reggie's new relationship, I remember spending a lot of time with my big sister and brother to. Mama and Reggie were working to secure us a roof over our head. They were once introduced to each other by my Aunt Loretta and soon after they were getting help from my Aunt Loretta to get the house they found off of 7mile in Detroit. Aunt Loretta was a major player in the real estate business back then so helping her big sister find a place where she could lay her head was a delight to Aunt Loretta.

My Mom and Reggie got married with only me and the Reverend present. When I was old enough to understand what really happened that day, I wasn't sure if God was actually present during their ceremony or not. As I began to grow older and mature in my faith I began to understand that

God doesn't make **ANY MISTAKES!** It was what it was, and it is what it is! I believe that everything is in Divine Order, everything happens for a reason. If it hadn't been for the things I've experienced, whether good or bad, I would not be the man that I am today.

The story that you're currently reading would not have been written. I believe that everything that we go through is not necessarily for us; it's for someone else that may need to see an example of how we get through it, and how to rely on God and take action to remove ourselves from a dark space. I give God all the Glory for helping me to get back on track time after time. If it hadn't been for the Lord by my side, I don't know where I would be right now.

Well we finally moved into a house over on Sussex off of Pembroke close to 7mile. It felt awkward getting used to my mom's last name changing from

Jackson to Grice. It was during this time when I attended Bow Elementary. I used to race kids home from school, but one particular time I remember racing a kid home while I was wearing my brown Buster Brown corduroy jacket and pants outfit with a pair of brown suede shoes.

After that race I thought I was unbeatable. I wanted to race everybody! Those suede dress shoes made me feel like I had bionic feet because they were so light. I thought I was just as fast as the roadrunner. To hear those corduroys whistle as I took off made it seem as if I was The Six Million Dollar Man or something. I was definitely feeling myself at that moment.

During this time Reggie's heroin addiction started to surface and we eventually ended up losing that house to. I was terrified in the house on Sussex at night when it was time to go to bed. Reggie would turn off all the lights and shut my door and theirs too. I hated that. I believed at that time that there was a monster in my closet and it was also one in the corner of my room on my chair.

One night I was left home alone while taking a bath and told not to get out of the tub until they got back from going to get us something to eat. The house was creaking and I thought someone was trying to get in to take me or kill me. I couldn't take it any longer. I knew if I got out of that tub I was gonna get a whoopin but the fear of being taken or killed was much greater than a butt whoopin.

I got out of the tub dripping water all the way to the phone in my mother and Reggie's room. I called my big brother William and begged him to come rescue me and this dude did just that. Will and one of his friends jumped on the bus and got there within an hour or so, the only thing is, they got there a little too late.

Mama and Reggie had returned and noticed wet footprints on the floor and they asked me did I get out the tube? I said "No I didn't." I was spared the butt whoopin for lying. They knew that something wasn't adding up. Finally I was dismissed from the interrogation and told to go to bed. As soon as I got into bed, my brother started banging on the front door.

My brother told my Mom and Reggie that I had called him crying and said that someone was trying to break in, which at the time I thought to be true.

Reggie tore my ass up that night and I was thinking to myself, "Why are ya'll allowing this dude to whip me like this." My Mom tried to get me to call him daddy Reggie at one time and I couldn't do it because it didn't feel right. There were times when Reggie would take me with him to visit his addict friends at their drug den homes and have me sit in the front room or go outside and play with the other kids that lived there or were there with their parents just like me. Reggie and his drug addict friends shot up heroin usually in the back rooms. I Hated Reggie with a passion but there was nothing I could do as a child to get my mother away from him, plus this dude was a loose cannon or should I say Coo Coo for Cocoa Puffs.

I remember staying with my Uncle "Top" and Aunt Dorothy on Littlefield off of Joy Road in Detroit very briefly. Uncle Top was one of my dad and moms best friends. I was almost a teenager before I realized that Uncle Top and Aunt Dorothy were not actually blood related. Before moving to Uncle Top and Aunt Dorothy's side of town I was attending Ilene Elementary on the west side of Detroit. Ilene Elementary is where I met my Dads mother for the first time that I could actually remember as a kid in my homeroom class. All my classmates knew who she was to me but I had no clue.

She came to our classroom and read us a story. Grandma was a school teacher and I had no idea. While at Ilene I experienced being the last student sitting on the playground waiting for my ride to come on many occasions. One day a teacher asked me was I okay and I told her "yes I'm okay, just waiting for my ride to come, they should be here in a minute." I said. I was taught that what goes on at home bet not get discussed outside our home, plus I didn't want to get in trouble for saying something I wasn't supposed to say, so I kept it short and sweet.

Eventually I was transferred to a school called McFarlane right off of Joy Road. I actually enjoyed being over there with my play cousins Charlie Brown and Debra. I still today remember running really fast and slipping in a large puddle of oil in their garage while wearing some of my good school clothes. I was covered with oil from head to toe and my cousin Charlie Brown thought it was hilarious. Living with them didn't last long. We began to live a life that resembled the life of gypsies moving from place to place.

We started living with my mom's close friend who she at one time worked with at the U.S Post

Office... her name was Pat. We began to live with Aunt Pat on 15th and Ferry Park on the west side of Detroit. I remember the time Pat told my mom that she and I could stay, but Reggie crazy ass had to go. It was during this time when I attended Woodward Elementary and attended the free lunch programs at a Catholic Church around the corner nearby. It was at that church around the corner where I lost my first pair of top front teeth. I was in a head on collision during a relay racing activity and collided with another kid's forehead, who by the way seemed unfazed by our collision.

After eventually being put out of Aunt Pat's house we moved into an apartment building called the Stanton on West Grand Boulevard right next to the Grocery store off of Linwood on the west side of Detroit. It was at this time when I remember going to stay with my dad more often on the weekends and for summer vacations at his place on Lawrence and Dexter on the west side of Detroit.

My dad lived in some type of boarding house

where he rented a room from a man that I considered to be like an Uncle named Steve. It was Steve who owned the property, a man named Mr. Red who rented a room and my Dad that lived there. These guys use to drink regularly but especially on the weekends. Our house was the hang out spot for those that liked to drink and party on the front porch with my Dad, Steve and Mr. Red. They would sit on the porch drinking, talking and laughing until someone was offended or angered by something that was said and then it was on like popcorn. My Dad used to fight almost every weekend and he was really good at it to.

Dudes did not want to get into a confrontation with my Dad because his deep voice alone was like the roar of a lion. He knew how to throw his hands too and I never seen him lose a fight. He would say in his loud roaring voice, "Nigga Put Yo Boots On" and it was on and poppin! My Dad picked me up to come stay with him one summer and when I walked in the door I didn't want to talk to Mr. Red who was sitting on the couch in front of me. Mr. Red asked me to shake his hand and I refused so he grabbed my arm and twisted it.

My play cousin Nikki witnessed what he had done and went in the kitchen and told my Dad immediately. My Dad came out of the kitchen and without any hesitation my dad punched Mr. Red straight in the face very hard. Mr. Red's face was bleeding and at that very moment I knew that my Dad did not play about me. After seeing Mr. Red's face get broke because he decided he wanted to twist my arm, I was terrified of getting a butt whipping from my Dad.

My Mom, Reggie and I eventually moved across the street from the Stanton apartment building into another apartment building called the Glen, which was also on the Boulevard off of Linwood. It was at that apartment building where I started seeing Reggie's heroin addiction start to get really out of control. People had to bring him home and drop him on the stoop because he was so damn high. Reggie came home one day after allegedly stabbing somebody. He had blood all over his hands and arm with the bloody butcher knife still in hand. Me and my mom where terrified. I knew for sure at that very moment that we were dealing with a mad man. He slapped my mother one day while I was present and I wanted to kill his ass but I was terrified of him and too small to defend my Mom.

Reggie's heroin addiction forced me to keeping a watch out for anything he was doing before he started a nod. Most of the time, I had to put out his cigarettes when he nodded off so he wouldn't burn down the house or apartment we were in. I also had to pee in pill bottles for him regularly so he could pass his drug test for probation or parole. I remember sitting in the front seat of our car with no seatbelts riding down the highway while watching Reggie go off into a nod.

That nod almost killed us because we could've been in a head on collision if I hadn't yelled at Reggie as loud as I did. If I hadn't hollered for dear life the way that I did, we would have definitely been ejected through the windshield and probably killed because we were traveling at a pretty high speed. Reggie had gone to sleep on me.

3: SCHOOL DAYS

W because I never had a chance to be hen in Elementary I hated school stable long enough to establish early childhood friends. I can remember a few kids but not many from elementary. I was very shy back then and we were constantly on the move from place to place. I did however establish some long lasting friendships when I finally moved with my dad for good in 1979 on Waverly right off of Dexter in Detroit.

A year or so before moving with my dad, we were still residing at The Glen Apartments on West Grand Blvd right off of Linwood. During this time my Granddaddy "T" became ill and was hospitalized. I remember going to see my Grandad at his house on St. Clair St between Shoemaker and the Edsel Ford Fwy also known as 94. I asked him one day during our visit with him could he buy me a mini bike and he said yes without hesitation. Granddaddy "T" was a hardworking man, but also was a hustler when it came to gambling. Pinochle was one of his favorite card games.

There were rumors back then that he had money hidden in the walls of his house. I was super excited about getting a mini bike, and I knew it was on the way because all he had to do is go in one of those walls and get some cash out to complete the deal. Soon after that night he became ill. I remember traveling down interstate 94 to go see Grandad in the hospital.

It was always tough for my mom. We passed the Uniroyal Giant Tire right off the highway in Allen Park going and coming from seeing Grandad every time. Grandad fought a good fight but eventually he passed away which devastated us all. A short time after Grandad passed; we received a telephone call late one night from a close friend who lived directly across the street from Grandad and Grandma Helen.

My mom answered the phone that night and the next thing you know she was letting out a loud scream saying NO LORD!!! Grandma Helen had died and was found in the bathroom of their home. Our family friends who were also neighbors across the street couldn't get her on the phone and she wouldn't answer the door either, so they knew for sure that something wasn't right. They communicated with her daily and would know if she was leaving because she would always let them know.

They decided to break down the door to see if she was okay, but soon after realized that she was unresponsive with no pulse. Grandma Helen had become sick almost immediately after Grandad had passed, and now she was gone only a short time afterward. Once Grandma Helen passed away, we left the apartment building and moved into my late Grandparents house.

To be honest, I really didn't want to move into their house because Grandma Helen had just died in there and I had already thought the house was Super Spooky, especially in the basement.

While living on the Eastside I attended William Robison Elementary School. I caught the yellow school bus everyday on the service drive of interstate 94. I was okay with the bus ride but I hated the school. I use to think I was the coolest every chance I got to walk through the halls with my new Jingle Boots jingling. My dad had just bought me the new popular boots while I visiting him on one of our weekend visits. All the cool kids were wearing Jingle Boots back then. The Principle however put an end to the jingle boot racket rather quickly by making us all buckle them up.

My homeroom teacher name was Mrs. Swarzoosky or something like. She was a pretty mean teacher and to make things worse she was literally cross eyed, which meant you never really knew if she was talking to you or someone else. She would catch us talking all the time because we never knew if she was actually looking at us.

Mrs. Swarzoosky told all the black boys one day that our schools policy forbids black boys to wear braids because it's sometimes hard to tell us apart from the girls. I was just a kid but somehow I knew that what she had just told us was racist and I didn't like it.

During one of the summer months while living on the Eastside, I was standing outside one day with my mom talking and she asked me to go to the corner store to break some food stamps by buying Koolaid. I didn't want anybody to see me with food stamps back then and what made this worse is the fact that I had to leave the store and come back again in order to break each one dollar food stamp. I would usually do this to get enough money to buy cigarettes. Well anyway, my mom told me not to ride my bike to the store because someone might steal it. I explained to her that I had ridden to the store several times before in the past and had no issues.

My mom was adamant about me not riding my bike but I was set on proving her wrong so I rode it anyway. I was only in the store a few minutes and when I came out my bike was gone with the wind. I was furious! I walked home thinking that my mom had something to do with it to teach me a lesson but that was not the case. Mama went off when I told her my bike was stolen. She wanted to kick my ass something terrible but she knew that I was already suffering enough so she gave me a pass.

I can recall vividly one night when Reggie demanded that my brother and his girlfriend stay with us for the night because they all had been drinking at a party that they had just returned from. My brother refused to stay so Reggie decided to run into the room to grab the rifle. He came out holding the rifle in his right hand with his finger close to the trigger.

He waved the gun in me and my nephew's direction when he first came out and then he pointed it in the direction of my mom, my brother and his girlfriend and all of a sudden we heard a loud bang. Everybody looked around wondering where the bullet went and then we noticed a trickle of blood starting to come out of my brother's girlfriend's pants leg.

She started to panic for a minute but she eventually calmed down and held it together considering her traumatic experience. Even though I couldn't stand Reggie at all, we all knew what he had done was accidental. Reggie had been drinking too, but that didn't excuse his reckless deadly behavior. That bullet could have killed anybody in that house, especially my brother's girlfriend after being shot. Reggie was a living nightmare!

4: SISTER LOVE

I remember going to stay with my sister for the summer on Hanna between 7 mile and Emery St on the Eastside. I always had a good time hanging with my big sister and brother and I would throw a fit if my brother stopped by and didn't take me with him. I knew for sure that my brother was the coolest dude on the planet back then. My sister was more like a second mom to me back then while I was growing up and she didn't take no stuff out of me or nobody else. She would speak her mind even if it meant hurting your feelings or pissing you off. Her oldest son my nephew Mike was my guy back then.

My sister used to let me take him for rides on her 10 Speed with the baby seat mounted on the back. I remember one time Mike and I were riding and without using any of my common sense, I tried to pop a Willy. All I gotta say is Thank the Lord for helping me to bring that front wheel back down to the ground because if I would have flipped all the way back, in which I almost did, I could have seriously injured or possibly even killed my nephew. I'm sure my sister would've killed me back then if God didn't help me bring that front wheel back down to the ground. I would've been devastated if that bike would've flipped all the way back. It totally scared the shit out of me! That was definitely a lesson well learned for me. To God Be the Glory for saving both of our lives that day.

During that summer at my sister's house, something transpired over the phone between her and my Dad that had her so angry that a blood vessel on her forehead was visible through the skin. She was "grit your teeth" angry! My Dad and Uncle Kenny came to get me and my uncle Kenny decided to let my sister know that a vein was protruding under the skin on her forehead. Of course that didn't help the situation one bit. Tensions were high that evening and I knew that whatever it was about it definitely had something to do with me. I believe I was beginning to become a burden on my sister. It was already enough for her to be raising her own child. Having to drag me along I'm sure was starting to become overwhelming to her. Around this time in my life I was all over the place. That night I ended up going with my dad for a few days but the days that followed, I traveled to my Aunt Ernie's and my Aunt Carol's.

After finally returning back to my sister's house and hoping that I could attend school from her house instead, I was told that I would be returning back home with my mom and Reggie to begin my new school year on the Eastside. Soon after I was told I had to return home to my mom and Reggie I was told that that it was a change in plans because the house had gotten broken into and all of my clothes and toys were stolen. I still today believe that Reggie took them and sold them to buy more drugs like he sold some of my other clothes my sister brought me.

When he sold my clothes he stated that the clothes my sister brought me were too grown for me. He then turned around and sold those same clothes to his sister for his nephew Paul that was the same age as me.

At this point I was not too happy with my mom for allowing all this crazy stuff to keep happening and I hated Reggie with a passion. It seemed like my mom was in some sort of daze with this guy and we all had become his hostages. My mom had been threatened by Reggie many times in the past and he told her he would harm her very badly or possibly even kill her if she tried to leave him. Based on some of the crazy things he's done in the past, I can understand why she believed him.

My dad wanted me to come live with him at his new place on Waverly off of Dexter and I was okay with that because I didn't want to have to deal with Reggie anymore. I was very familiar with the Dexter and Linwood area because my Grandma and grandad lived on Leslie and Dexter; my dad had lived on Lawrence and Dexter. I also remember living on Rochester and Dexter briefly with my mama and Reggie. I also remember riding with Reggie back in the days before I moved with my Dad and stopping on Dexter and

Richton at the apartment building over the store to cop his dope or to sell whatever pills he had to sell.

Reggie sold T's and Blues or Tylenol 4's mainly but he would sell whatever that made him some money. Reggie was definitely a hustler with a gift of gab with a temper that would go from zero to one hundred in a matter of seconds. It was at this same apartment building where Reggie shot a dude in the face for something they had a disagreement about. Reggie was a dangerous man!

5: DEAR DAD

I start the 6 grade at Longfellow Middle School on finally got moved in with my dad and was ready to the Westside of Detroit. My very first day at my dad's house was a violent one. I was sitting at the dining room table eating my two piece meal from Church's Chicken and the next thing I know, my dad's girlfriend Brenda picked up a chair and slammed it over my dad's head. Before I knew it my dad was up and scrappin with this big strong motorcycle gang woman.

We had wood floors which made the sound of their fight sound like an earthquake or something. The house literally sounded like it was two big giants fighting. Violence was a guaranteed event that took place at 2903 Waverly on Fridays and Saturdays. My dad and our neighbors that lived upstairs in the two-family flat would invite friends and family over to party, drink liquor, smoke weed, listen to music and talk about old times. They would drink and talk stuff all night upstairs until there was a disagreement about something.

I would sometimes be a nervous wreck when I would hear my dad upstairs arguing with somebody. My dad would fight at the drop of a dime. The first time I seen him fight was when he lived on Lawrence off of Dexter. He punched a dude named Red in the face for twisting my arm because I didn't want to shake his hand. There was another time when somebody stole my bike from Sheba's Beer & Wine Store on Davidson between Dexter and Wildermere while I was inside buying candy. I had to walk home to tell my dad about my bike getting stolen only to regret telling him because he went and grabbed his rifle and had his friend drive us through the neighborhood looking for my bike and the person that stole it.

I prayed to God that we didn't find the person who stole it because I didn't want my dad to kill or hurt anybody over a bike that was at the least 6 to 7 years old. I was ready for a new bike anyway. To make a long story short, my dad did not play when it came to me, our family or anything else that was under his watch. My dad had the skin of an Armadillo and the heart of a Lion. There was also another side to him that was very caring, loving and giving. My dad was a good man.

Moving in with my dad is where I finally had the chance to establish some friendships that are stronger today than they were back then. At Longfellow Middle School Mr. Halton was my homeroom teacher and he was also our gym teacher. This is the school where I began hanging out with the bad kids. Mr. Halton used to always tell me that if I kept hanging with the bad kids I was going to end up in jail or pushing daisies. I paid him no attention whatsoever and began my journey of becoming a neighborhood thug!

I was a little bitty guy and I wasn't the strongest or the toughest in the neighborhood but I definitely held my own. If I had a problem with somebody and couldn't handle it alone I would get some of my guys from Dexter or Linwood to beat whoever it was up which didn't help me at all with taming my big mouth. There was one time when I bussed through this dude I didn't like and two girls that were all walking down the hallway hugged up.

I thought I was a bad ass because of the guys I hung out with. I thought I was a beast or something and got knock straight down to the floor by the guy I was trying to bully. Mr. Halton witnessed it and told me to get my ass up, get to class and told me I needed to quit trying to be a little bad ass. After school that day, my homeboy TC punched the guy who knocked me down in the face with a padlock. I never had an issue out of that guy ever again after that.

I remember the first time I had ever heard of YBI (Young Boy's Inc.) it was after getting my army hat snatched by Michael Miller & Samirone Brown (Lil Teddy). They followed me all the way home from school one day just to take my hat. They asked me did I know somebody down the street and pointed.

When I turned my head in the direction that they were pointing, they snatched my hat and ran. I chased them until Mike Miller turned around and got into a

Kung Fu stands as if he was Bruce Lee or something. I had company that day on my porch and they went to tell my dad.

My dad came out and asked me did I know the guys who took my hat and I said yup.

I hate I ever told my dad because he called the school and found out where they lived and took me down there to get my hat. I got my hat back minus all the fake gold chains I had added to it. The next time I seen Teddy who eventually became Butch's lieutenant in the YBI, was when he came up to Longfellow to show his face and to drop out of school. He was dope boy fresh with a beige leather Max Julian coat with real fur around the collar and a pocket full of money. During that time I was walking to school in tennis shoes with holes at the bottom. I was wondering to myself, "What can I do to dress like that."

I eventually began hanging with one of Teddy's little brothers Dre which lead to me getting my first pair of hand-me-down Top Tens. Dre let me wear his original blue and white Top Tens and those babies were funky! Dre was wearing them without socks which made them sweaty and funky. I didn't care though because I just wanted to dress and be respected like the big drug dealers in my neighborhood. I eventually had to give those shoes back but Dre turned around and gave me a pair of white and silver low top double strap Top Tens that I eventually customized to bring them back to life. I got the idea to customize Adidas Top Tens from my good friend Mark Gardner aka Big Ace who was the first that I know of in our hood or any hood to customize a pair of Top Tens.

6: TEMPTATION

To look good for the girls in school, he temptation was weighing in very heavy so I began selling drugs periodically when I was able to get away from the house long enough without my dad realizing I was several blocks away. I sold drugs back then either on Dexter or Linwood for cash to play video games and to help me buy clothes and shoes to look good for the girls and let everybody else know that I was getting a few dollars hustling.

My dad didn't believe in spending more than $30 on a pair of sneakers and $30 was actually pushin it. He would always reference a pair of sneakers that he bought over 11 years ago during that time and would look proud while he explained to me the condition of his shoes and how good they looked. It was during this time when I decided I wanted to be like the money getters in my hood. I looked up to the dope dealers that were riding around in expensive cars or Renegade Jeeps with the tops off wearing Donkey Kong gold rope chains, Adidas Top Tens, Adidas track suits, silk shirts, fine women and pockets full of money. These guys during this time in my life were my role models. I wanted to be just like them. This is the time when I started hanging with all of my bad homies in the hood and doing whatever it took to come up on some cash.

We sold drugs and stole cars just to joyride around the hood and pull up on girls we knew, but most of the time we would strip the cars we stole to sell the parts for pennies on a dollar. By 9th grade I had become completely corrupted and had no interest in attending classes after I had gotten so far behind from skipping class. I did however love going to school just to see the girls. When most were going to school in the morning I was going to the stroll to sell heroin. Scanning the area for police and dope fiends became second nature.

We took turns on who was gonna be the lookout and who was gonna get the top money off of each pack of dope we sold. I had seen a very lot of money being raked in off the streets and I had made a decision that being a drug dealer long-term would work as long as I was careful. That didn't work out at all! On my first day of attending Central High School off of Linwood and Tuxedo on Detroit's westside I decided that I was gonna be a full fledge Dexter Boy, which meant if another Dexter Boy or NFL (Niggaz From Linwood) had an issue with anybody, that issue had just became my issue as well.

Back then we were having issues with different cats from different hoods, not to mention the issues we had with the opposing team to YBI aka Young Boys Incorporated. That opposing team was called the Pony Down Crew! This new lifestyle that I had chosen led me to drinking and drugging daily.

I eventually started lacing my marijuana with cocaine to merely fit in. I have to admit that I was also curious about cocaine because of the stories I had heard about some of the real money getters going to concerts lacing their weed with cocaine. This was the drug for those that were getting major money from what I was told.

I had made a very bad decision to join in on something that I know has changed the trajectory of where my life would've ended up, but I guess we'll never truly know how my life would've turned out if I would've went in another direction. Regardless of how my life has turned out, I believe that everything is in divine order. God's plan was laid out. I believe that everything I went through throughout my life was not necessarily for me but for someone that needs to hear my story and how God restored me to sanity.

Unfortunately I was the one who decided to travel on that road to nowhere, I was the one who decided to travel on a road to complete self-destruction if I wasn't stopped. If it hadn't been for the Lord by my side and His Mercy and Grace I would not have made it thus far. There was a time when things began to turn bad for me and I began to blame those that offered me my 1st round of marijuana laced with cocaine.

Today I understand that they were just as sick as I was, and although I may have not been responsible for my addiction, I am however responsible for my recovery. It took me many years afterwards to understand this concept.

At the age of 16 years old I ran away from home because I didn't want to abide by my dad's rules. I also got tired of getting yelled at when my dad got drunk and hearing his threats that we were gonna fight if I messed up again. I hid out for 2 day's straight a few doors down the street from our house at my best friends Pat & Quentin's house in their basement. Eventually I started couch surfing from one house to another. I went to my Aunt Carol's house and spent the night and that night turned in to a couple of weeks. My Aunt Carol got my dad on the phone one day so I could speak with him and he asked me to come home but I told him I didn't want to come home. I was done with receiving the verbal abuse every time he got drunk.

My sister finally agreed to take me in after I decided not to return home to my dad. Living with my sister, my brother-in-law, two nephews and a niece was a great experience and one of the best times in my life that I will never ever forget, but back then the urge to get out and hustle was still in me and I was going to get it one way or another.

I worked a lot of fast food jobs while living with my sister but I hated working in fast food with a passion. I eventually got caught carrying a concealed weapon, which I only carried for my protection because I had gotten robbed at gun point a few times prior. It had gotten so bad in Detroit that when dudes would rob you, they would also shoot you even after you gave them what they wanted to keep you from coming back to retaliate. I had made up in my mind that I would rather be judged by twelve then carried by six. Detroit had gotten so bad that you had to keep your head on a swivel if you were riding in a nice whip and dressed to impress.

If you looked like money you were a target.

After being motivated by my cousin Darlene who always used to tell the drug dealers in the hood to get a job and Get a G.E.D. or Do Somethin' was her consistent message while we served custo's in front of her all through the day and night on Prairie St on

Detroit's westside. Her persistent rant "Get a job, Get a G.E.D, Do Somethin" sparked something in me one day and made me decide to go back to school to get my G.E.D.

I dropped out of high school in the 11th grade because schools in Detroit had become very dangerous for me since I had gotten kicked out of my neighborhood school (Detroit Central High School). I also attended Northwestern High and Northern High and eventually got kicked out of those schools as well. Gangs in other areas knew how guys from Dexter dressed, who we were with and how we got down. I was a walking target and also associated with Dexter Boys and Young Boys Inc.

I attended The Detroit Youth Foundation on the westside of Detroit and finally received my G.E.D. I decided to do something different with my life after getting caught with drugs and then right after that getting caught with a gun. I signed up for Job Corp and was accepted and rode the Greyhound bus to Indianapolis, Indiana and attended Job Corp in Edinburgh, Indiana where I lived for 2 years. I completed the Carpentry trade and got my first job in Detroit as a Carpenter's Apprentice helping to build the

Comerica Building that's located in downtown Detroit. That same building is now called the Ally Detroit Center.

Unfortunately though, while working for this construction company that actually gave me the job the first day I stepped on the sight, I caught another carrying a concealed weapons charge that ended my career there fast. My uncle Philip, former manager for the Motown group the Spinners and other well-known artist that were a part of Motown had become the right hand man to City Councilman Gil Hill. He did everything in his power to get me out of trouble. My judge showed me leniency based on my Uncle Philip and City Councilman Gil Hills plea to give me another chance.

My Judge sentenced me to 2 years' probation with 6 months on a tether. I was okay with the probation but the tether I just couldn't do so I skipped town and went back to Job Corp because my living situation at home was horrible at the time and I needed a fresh start somewhere else. I re-signed up for Job Corp in Edinburgh Indiana and they took me back in and allowed me to take up another trade.

When I completed the trade and graduated, I was relocated to Nashville Tennessee for a position as a Plasterer in the cement masonry field. I had two roommates, one from Chicago and the other from Los Angeles California. This was the fresh start that I needed. The country sites, the mountains, the view of the top of trees for miles from my apartment balcony looked so very appealing especially compared to how I was living in Detroit.

In my hood we didn't see nothing but crackheads, crack houses, liquor stores and winos. I felt good being in a different environment and around people that would pull up to you at the stop light and throw up the peace signs and actually speak. We didn't do that in Detroit, but it felt good to see people that looked like me speak instead of mean muggin which could sometimes lead to shots fired.

7: LOVE ARRIVES

In 1991 when I moved to Nashville Tennessee. Met my wife Chantelle for the very first time I also met a very good friend named Vickie that same year. Vickie and I dated briefly before I met Chantelle and we remained friends afterwards. Back then, whichever girl I hung out with on any given night was usually based on who was available. I was a True Player back then and there was only one thing that I was interested in. This was actually the first time I lived in Tennessee before returning to Detroit for a while because we couldn't pay our rent.

My roommate and I had fallen behind on our rent because of mismanaging our money and getting rained out multiple days in a two week period at our job.

We couldn't lay cement or dryvit in the rain which also meant we didn't get paid either. I returned home to Detroit only to realize how much I wanted to get back to Tennessee. Chantelle had reached out to me in Detroit a few times and told me she was pregnant by me, so I was doing everything that I could to get back to Tennessee as quickly as possible. I was definitely okay with her having my child. I wanted my own and I was prepared to do whatever it took to take care of our child.

After finally making it back to Tennessee, I met with Chantelle only to find out that she had been lying to me about her pregnancy. She admitted lying to me only because she wanted me to come back to be with her. She also talked about moving to Detroit to be with me if I didn't want to return to Tennessee. I had no solid place to stay when I returned to Nashville but I was hoping that I could shack up with one of my ex- roommates who was still living there. One of my good friends from Chicago, Demetrius Robinson aka Pops suggested that I go stay with another good friend of ours from Chicago named Tyrone Lott. Ty lived on the other side of town and had a roommate named Cory from Georgia.

Both Ty and Cory agreed to let me stay with them and that's when the weekend party shenanigans began! After living with Ty and Cory for a few months Ty told me that he had something to tell me. We eventually talked and he told me that Chantelle asked him to tell me that she was pregnant by the guy she dated before her and I had ever met. I was devastated because I really had strong feelings for her. I was angry at her because she told my roommate instead of telling me directly.

There was a part of me that still wanted to be with her but there was also a part of me that didn't want anything to do with her because she was about to have some other dudes baby. At this point, Ty and Cory and I were on the brink of getting put out of our apartment if we had one more incident.

That one more incident took place on a Friday evening after work. At least 30 to 40 people showed up to our party and acted a damn fool. There was drinking, smoking, fighting, sex and plenty of people hanging out in the parking lot at our apartment complex. Almost all of our neighbors filed a complaint and the police were definitely called to shut us down. This party was much worse than the pool party we had recently had that was filled with plenty of alcohol, marijuana and a whole lot of skinny dipping in our apartment complex community pool.

I had gotten back in touch with Vickie and told her my roommates and I were getting put out. She suggested that I move in with her at some new apartment complex she was looking at and we could split the rent. Considering the fact that I really had nowhere else to go at the time I accepted her offer and we became a low key couple. Vickie's mother was deep into the Church and she didn't believe in shacking up at all, so I had to hide whenever she stopped by unannounced. My roommates and I were straight up drunks, so transitioning over to having a woman as a roommate was definitely what was needed for me to put some balance back in my life.

She was clean, neat and she was good at preparing well balanced meals the way that my sister had done so well in the past. Vickie and I were tight but I knew that Vickie was not the woman that I wanted to spend the rest of my life with. I knew that Vickie would one day make a good wife to some good man but I knew that it wasn't gonna be me. I still had my heart set on Chantelle to the point where I would even stop by Chantelle's house with Vickie in the car. I was so very disrespectful back then but I didn't care at the time because my complete focus was on how I could get Chantelle back.

One day I was hanging out with Ty and Eric at Hadley Park on a Sunday afternoon and Ty had noticed Vickie pulling into the Wendy's parking lot where the parks overflow usually ended up. We all watched Vickie exchanging phone numbers with some dude standing over her driver's side door while she sat inside smiling and giggling. I walked up on her soon after the dude walked away and asked her what she was doing. She lied repeatedly so I decided that I was moving out of the apartment we both shared and I was going back to Detroit. I had no plans of staying in Detroit but I was homesick and really just trying to figure out a way to get away from Vickie.

I had an 86 Buick LeSabre back then. I packed it up that night and hit the highway the next following day, but not before stopping by to see

Chantelle before I left. I told Chantelle that I still wanted her but I had to go back to Detroit to take care of something and I would be back. Chantelle didn't seem as interested in us getting back together but she did hear me out. I wanted this girl very badly but I knew it wasn't gonna be easy.

I had made it back to Detroit and was there for at least a month. Vickie was pretty persistent on trying to reconcile our relationship, and by that time I was really ready to go back to Tennessee because things at home were bad. Vickie and I agreed upon getting back together to finish out the least, but I was just ready to get the hell out of Detroit. Vickie would call and talk to my mom a lot while I was not at home and one day she decided she wanted to travel to Detroit to meet my mom. We both agreed that she would arrive on a Saturday and we would drive back to Tennessee that following Monday or Tuesday.

The day after Vickie arrived to Detroit, she died of a Bronchial Asthma Attack. I was devastated, and at this point in my life I was very depressed because I had just lost a good friend and nothing else seemed to have been going right for me. I was in a very bad place and my only solution was to fill my body with chemicals to help me forget about everything. Calling Vickie's mom to tell her that her baby girl had died a day after we had just talked to her mom was the hardest thing I've ever attempted to do in my entire life.

My sister had to take the phone and tell Vickie's mom the bad news because I couldn't bear telling her mom such devastating news about her only daughter. All I could hear was Vickie's mom hollering through the phone when my sister broke the bad news to her. Some of her family members didn't know what to think, and some were wondering if I had something to do with her sudden death. All of the unanswered questions and the anger that her family felt led her mom to suggesting that I not come to the funeral. She stated that she didn't want anything else to happen and begged me not to show up.

Vickie's mom knew that based on the family not really knowing what happened to Vickie, it would be a serious problem if I had showed my face. I was completely devastated because I knew that this was so very far from the truth. I had made up in my mind that I was gonna go to the funeral anyway but my mom begged me not to go. Her mom also had reemphasized that she didn't want me there so I honored her wishes.

I was so very angry and so very hurt that anyone would think such a thing about me, but based on our break up, and me being a Detroit Bad Boy, they didn't know what to believe, especially since we were just on the phone the day before laughing with her mom. The few family members of Vickie that knew me knew that I was not capable of doing anything to harm Vickie.

At this point, I had started drinking and drugging on a regular bases. I eventually delved back off into smoking crack cocaine laced over marijuana or tobacco rolled up in cigarette papers. I had completely lost my mind to the point that I decided to rob my mom's landlord so I could continue buying more drugs. I was at a point of no return and didn't care if I lived or died. I had definitely hit rock bottom!

8: BAD DECISION

I was completely out of my mind from smoking t was the hot summer month of July 1993. I tobacco laced with crack cocaine rolled up in cigarette papers. We called this dangerous combination 51's back in those days. I was living with my mom at the time and she was usually at work during the day. I had been smoking 51's to the point where I had started pawning anything I had of value that the dope man or the pawn shop would take. I had just smoked the last of the dope I had which had me stuck and sitting there paranoid trying to figure out a way to go get more.

I needed to make this happen before my mom got home but time was running out. I heard our Landlord coming in through the back door of the two-family flat we resided in. They proceeded walking up the back stairwell. I peeked out and asked if I could borrow some money but was told "no." Our Landlord expressed that they didn't have any money to loan, but of course I didn't believe them and I wasn't taking no for an answer. I began to conjure up a ridiculous crack head story to try to convince our Landlord that I really needed the money only to get denied once again. I knew that she had some money in that house and I was determined to find it even if I had to tie her up so I could search the house to find it, plus I didn't want her to call the police or run and get a gun to shoot me. I just wanted the money to go buy more drugs, nothing more, and nothing less.

The drugs had me so gone that I wasn't even concerned about any consequences. I was trapped in the grips of a very bad addiction that wanted me dead.

During the robbery my Landlord shouted, "Father forgive him for he know not what he do." I stopped in my tracks for a second, but the compulsion to get more drugs had me in a stronghold that was much stronger than what I could conquer on my own. I was spiritually bankrupt. I was not in my right state of mind. Crack Cocaine had me caught up in a cycle of addiction that was very difficult for me to break free from. I was not myself when I committed this senseless crime but I must say that I did know better because I was raised better. I take full responsibility for what I did regardless of the state of mind that I was in. What I did was wrong and I needed to be punished for what I had done.

I chose to get high that day when I knew how cunning and baffling crack cocaine was. Committing this crime was the worst decision I've ever made in my life. Not only because I was going to jail, but also because I disrupted someone's life the way that I did and completely went against my own morals and principles by robbing from the elderly . This was the worst day of my life, and I was hoping and praying that this was all just a bad dream. However, this was not a bad dream; this was reality setting in with severe consequences that would shortly follow.

That bad decision cost me 9 to 20 years in the Michigan Department of Corrections. I had just graduated to the big leagues and had no idea how I was gonna do all this time. I started off at the Jackson State Penitentiary in Jackson Michigan, and then I was transferred to the Upper Peninsula at the Chippewa Correctional Facility. While at this facility I finally received a letter from Vickie's mom stating that the autopsy had come back and she was relieved to inform me and everyone else that Vickie died from natural causes (Bronchial Asthma Attack). She was so very sorry that she denied me the opportunity to be at the funeral for her daughter.

She knew that Vickie and I were very tight and she knew Vickie would've wanted me to be there to. I cried like a baby when I read that letter but still felt angry inside because people had come to a conclusion about me without knowing the facts. I eventually got over it as time went by because anger is too heavy a load to carry. Vickie was a very special girl with a generous heart. She had my best interest at heart and was a true friend from the very first time I met her up until her untimely demise.

While serving time behind the walls I got involved in any and every positive program that the Michigan Department of Corrections had to offer. I was ready to go home from the very first day I set foot behind those Penitentiary gates. My dad died soon after on December 30th 1994. I was devastated but even more so because I was not allowed to go to his funeral and say my final goodbyes. I was very angry at the officers that denied my request and I was also angry at my counselor for not doing a better job at trying to get me to my dad's funeral.

A few weeks later my counselor had me shipped to the Muskegon Correctional Facility which was much closer to Detroit. I wasn't there long before receiving more bad news that my Aunt Evelyn had passed away and a short time after, my Grandmother passed away as well. I had made up in my mind that I was NOT gonna let anything else stop me from being the man that I knew my dad wanted me to be. I was determined to turn my life around and prove to any and every one that I was worth a second chance.

While serving time at the Muskegon Correctional Facility I became friends with a small circle of brothers that had the same or similar goals that I had.

One goal that we all had in common of course was regaining our freedom! We all knew that there was a better way and we were all determined to align ourselves in the direction of where we needed to go to reach those goals. We walked for miles in circles on the prison yards back forty discussing our future plans of getting out, reuniting with our families and getting rich.

We encouraged each other daily and reminded each other that we were unique and not like all the rest. We believed that we stood out and we also believed that we would stand a better chance at breaking into the music industry based on our artists talent and our connection with Jason who just so happened to be the brother of Hip Hop Artist/Actor Alvin Joiner aka Xzibit. We knew that we could make it happen on our own but we also knew that the process could move a lot faster once we got the opportunity to connect with a major artist that could ultimately walk us in the door to a major label.

Jason assured us all that he would handle plugging us in once we all started to get released and we all took his word for it. We were all fascinated with the art of hip hop music and the potential profits it could bring in if we had the right team of contributors to help bring it into fruition. Just so happen, we had the perfect team of individuals who were hungry enough to do whatever it took to get to where we were all striving to go. We had plans of taking over the hip hop industry by storm "Seriously!"

The number one rap artist on the yard at the Muskegon Correctional Facility in the mid to late 1990's was Seven The General and he was signed to Dymond Entertainment. I knew Seven before prison and was completely surprised to see him walking into the prison restroom one day as I was walking out. This guy could imitate Tony Montana from Scarface and sound exactly like the movie.

Seven's ability to rhyme and perform on stage

made him a celebrity on the yard. Any and everybody in their right mind knew that Seven was going places in the rap game once he got released from prison and Dymond Entertainment was the label that was going to deliver him to the place where we all wanted him to be.

We all wanted to get into the industry and get money like Roc-A-Fella Records. Dymond Entertainment had three equal share owners which consisted of Jason as CEO, Greg as President and myself as Executive Vice President. AJ was an employee of Dymond Entertainment and served as our VP of Operations. Greg's mom helped us tremendously by going out to obtain the necessary documents we needed to establish our company. Some didn't understand and wondered "How you gonna start a business in jail?" We did not listen to any of the negative rhetoric and we would not be denied. We even had one of our counselors notarize a few documents after Jay, Greg and I signed on the dotted line.

We also established a publishing company named **Create A Way Publishing**. We were all very serious about the road we all had chosen to travel. Everybody had a position to play and Greg was a major key to our progress. For starters Greg had already ran a business on the streets before coming to prison so he was already familiar with certain formalities to get the process started. Greg was well disciplined in prison when it came to reading, studying and overall personal growth, Greg was much focused. Greg was able to consolidate our ideas and include them into the business plan that he so brilliantly prepared on a $100 Brother typewriter. Greg was a doer which made him a great business partner to work with.

Jason's position as CEO was not given to make him the shot caller over Greg and I, but to put him in position to represent us when it was time for him to speak with his brother. Again we were all equal share owners. Jason's position was positioned to put us into position. Jason's biggest task was to fulfill his commitment by plugging us in directly with his brother so he could walk us in the door to the majors to display our talent. My position demanded a lot of reading and learning the business along with marketing, promoting and helping Greg with anything that was needed to help our business grow. I put together a proposal at the Muskegon Correctional Facility to MC a talent show with Seven The General aka The Black Duncan McCloud and Lil Boo aka Meethose aka Funkanees aka The Shogun as the headliner.

Seven and Lil Boo aka Fastlane tore the house down! We were all inches away from being put on lock down and I was told that no more shows would be approved. The whole auditorium of inmates lost their damn minds that day. Seven spit some bars referencing signs and symbols that described The Moorish Science Temple and Islam and every brother in the auditorium got up out of their seats roaring and clapping for the dynamic duo on. That performance was definitely one for the history books. Another one of my positions was to be our videographer for Dymond Entertainment. I was blessed with the opportunity to get involved in an industry that would also help us to become more self- sufficient in recording and producing our own music and video content.

I graduated from a 2 year Television Production class on the third year. Our instructor Charlie was out sick for almost a year after suffering a ruptured appendix while at work in his classroom. Charlie eventually recovered from that health scare and returned to work. Finally for graduation I was able to send copies of my 3 commercials home and we made sure we sent one to Alvin. The commercials I produced were 10, 30 and 60 second commercials. The 60 second commercial was a Source Magazine commercial featuring Jason, Greg, Seven, C-Note and featured images of Tupac, Karl

Kani, Lil Kim, Xzibit, Wu Tang Clan and the cover of Source Magazines latest addition at the time.

Word on the yard was that the Michigan Department of Corrections was overcrowded and inmates that had already served a certain percentage of their time may get shipped to Jarrett Virginia to be housed for one year. Jason and I were two of the many that were shipped almost 700 miles away from our families in Detroit. The Greensville Correctional Center where we were housed was also where death row inmates served their last days. The Execution Chamber was very active while we were there. Several executions took place during the one year we were there.

During an execution they would lock the entire facility down for several hours if not the entire day. When someone would get executed they would ask them what they wanted for their last meal and most of the time the selection would be fried chicken, which was also a delicacy in most prisons in the USA. I hated this prison because with all of the people that had been wrongfully convicted of crimes they didn't do, who's to say that each time they executed someone that it was actually the right person.

Some inmates had become so desensitized that I heard a dude yell out "I wish they hurry up and kill a nigga so we can have some chicken." That made me so very angry and I knew then that we black folks got some serious issues. Deep down in my soul I knew that this prison shit was not for me and I wanted to get out and never ever come back. The very bad choice that I had made to get me in prison became a lesson well learned each and every day I did time in prison!

It was at this facility where I met Bernard Platter. Bernard was the person responsible for helping me create our new logo design. This guy is one of the coldest graphic designers on the planet. I gave him a rough draft of what I wanted and he brought it to life with some color pencils and some rulers. After discussing the need for the change with Greg via mail and Jason on the yard, we agreed that we needed to figure out a different acronym for our original name DIAMOND INC, which stood for Dominance Illustrates Aggressive Minds Operating On Non-Violent Decisions. Bernard and I sat down at a table to brainstorm on a new logo and I realized that if I spelled Diamond with a "Y" instead of an "I" we could create something that would not only bring value, but also not be a contradiction of the words that would eventually proceed out of the mouths of our rap artist.

While all this was taking place in Jarrett Virginia, Greg, D-World, Seven and Face Assassin was at MCF recording an album. Greg did an amazing job with organizing everything while Jason and I were in Virginia by getting our music producer D-World to lay the beats and do what no one had ever done before us at that facility! We were all excited about our future and Dymond Entertainment was now the new name of our company and the acronym stands for Dare Your Mind to Observe New Destinies!

9: FINDING FREEDOM

While serving time in Prison I knew for sure that I didn't want to return home the same way that I went in. I would sit on my bunk daily reflecting back to what led me to serving a 9 to 20 year prison sentence. There were times when I said to myself "I don't wanna be remembered as a junkie or crackhead doing stupid shit that jeopardizes my freedom, my sanity, my relationships, and even more importantly, my life." I became determined to change my life for the better. My plan was to become a better man, a better son to my mom, a better brother to my siblings including my step sisters Lekeysha and Mikita whom I also love dearly.

One day I decided to call my good friends Kris and Kelly from the westside of Detroit to say hello. Back in the day Kris and Kelly reminded me so much of the rap group Salt-N-Pepa. These two had the hairdos, the 8 Ball Jackets, the Puffed big gold earrings and the attitudes to match.

We had some really great times hanging at their house on Monte Vista back in the day. They answered my call that day and then all of a sudden Kelly dropped something on me that really made me think.

She said; "We need you to stay out the way in there, stay out of trouble, soak up as much knowledge as you can while you're in there and bring it home to us." That made me think really hard about what type of knowledge I wanted to take in so I could take it home. I knew at that moment that the best knowledge for me to soak up was the knowledge of self.

I was once told by a wise man that what we deposit is what we withdraw, so I knew that the best knowledge for me needed to come from God. That request that Kelly made also challenged me to really take a look at the role that I needed to play and the shoes that I needed to fill to lead my family in the right direction. My dad taught me to be a leader and not a follower, an asset and not a liability. It became my passion to change my life for the better so I intentionally started getting involved in any and every positive program that the Michigan Department of Corrections had to offer.

I went to prison because I had completely lost

control. I was battling against some demons that didn't wanna let go. The bible say's; "For we do not wrestle against flesh and blood, but against the rulers, against the authorities, against the cosmic power over this present darkness, against the spiritual forces of evil in the heavenly places" Ephesians 6:12 ESV.

I got caught up in a very dangerous choke hold with crack cocaine and it almost cost me my life, But God! If I could turn back the hands of time there are so many things that I would've done differently. For one, I never would've committed such a crime, and two, I would've never experimented with a drug that would one day become so addictive that I would actually consider robbing someone to get more. Considering the fact that I can't turn back the hands of time, I have to rely on my faith to remind me that God is in control. I believe that everything that happens, happens for a reason. My Mom would always say to me that everything is in divine order. There were times when I couldn't stand my Mom for saying that, it would make me cringe to think that God would allow bad things to happen, but over the years I began to realize and understand that God knows what's going to happen, when it's going to happen, and who's going to make it happen before it ever happens.

There is a lesson in any and everything that

happens. The thing is, will we actually learn from what we experience whether it's good or bad? I believe that everything I went through or put others through was not in vain. God has a plan for my life, and this is the very reason why Satan has been trying to destroy me from the time I was conceived.

It was required by the courts for me to attend Substance Abuse programming, but the courts didn't have to tell me I had a problem, I knew I had a problem and I was willing to do whatever it took to fix it and change my life forever. It was people like Doc Blue who came in as a volunteer to teach

Personal Growth and Substance Abuse Counselor Michael Johnson who helped to sharpen me along the way. Michael Johnson once said; "When you're out there getting high and get extremely paranoid as if someone's out to get you or kill you, it's actually death looking for you, that's why you can't figure it out."

That resonated very well with me and spooked me to my core. I started attending a countless number of substance abuse meetings and classes to help me understand my addiction and the deadly cycle of addiction that I had been trapped in for years leading up to my arrest on July 8th, 1993. After I became committed to attending any and every meeting that focused on personal growth and recovery, I was afforded the opportunity to facilitate some 12 step meeting groups and a few Big Book study groups as well. I eventually moved up to facilitating Substance Abuse phases 1, 2 and 3 to my fellow inmates and I also served as a volunteer Chairman for regular AA and NA meetings held inside the Muskegon Correctional Facility.

It was during this time when I started to

experience a true freedom within while still serving time behind bars. I also decided to become a member of the

National Lifers Association although I wasn't serving a life sentence. I joined the Lifer's Group because they were well disciplined brothers that focused on getting out of prison and challenging the system when policies and procedures seemed unfair or inhumane. Some facilities had programing that would provide the necessary tools for inmates to rehabilitate themselves, but there were also facilities (or particular officers) out there that would rather keep a knee on your neck rather than help you get out and stay out.

Some of my lifer brothers were attorney's that just hadn't had the opportunity to take the Bar Exam yet. These guys were well organized, very knowledgeable about the law and would fight for our rights as prisoners with dedication and a very strong conviction. This is what made me really want to get involved with the Lifer's Organization. It was within this organization where I was introduced to Mr. Tom J. Adams and Ms. Jessica Taylor from the Chance for Life Program based out of Detroit Michigan.

Tom and Jessica have played a major role with mentoring me and being a strong support base that I could always count on when things got tough or just to celebrate with me when things were going well. They told me that they would be there for me when it was time for me to make my transition back into society.

I would soon find out if their word was actually bond or if they were just saying what they thought I wanted to hear. A short time after I found out that their actions were just as solid as their words. Having a strong circle of support is a must when being released from prison, because there will be times when an encouraging word or a helping hand will go a long way. Sometimes just having someone to listen is all that it takes to get you through a very bad day.

10: RELEASED

I of Corrections on December 4 th 2001 and was released from the Michigan Department extradited to Nashville Tennessee to serve time for a theft of property-burglary charge I caught in February 1993. I was extradited prior to that in 1996 while still serving time at the Muskegon Correctional Facility on a Writ of Habeas Corpus. I was tried, convicted and sentenced to serve 2 years at 30 percent in the Tennessee Department of Corrections to be served after I completed serving my time in Michigan.

I was then transported back to the MDOC but

was pretty upset to know that they gave me consecutive time rather than running my time concurrent. I had no idea at the time that this would actually work out in my favor once I was released. In Tennessee I only had approximately 3 months to serve which turned out to be 85 days exact. When I was released from the Tennessee Department of Corrections on February 28th 2002 my soon to be wife picked me up in a 2000 brand new Black limited addition Toyota 4Runner SUV that she had financed for me because she knew that in order for me to get a job and maintain it, I needed to have my own reliable transportation to get me back and forth to work daily.

We both discussed our shared responsibilities upon my release and agreed that as long as I could pay my car note of a little over $500 a month, she could continue handling the rest of the bills for at least three months until I got a full-time job and built up a small savings to begin contributing more and investing in Dymond Entertainment.

I have to admit that I felt like the prodigal son

returning home. I left the streets a complete mess, but now my confidence level to succeed was very high. I was truly blessed to have a successful woman desire having me in her life considering where I was coming from. There was no doubt in my mind that this woman truly did love me for me and not for what I could provide for her at that moment.

Chantelle and I had our wedding date set for June 2002 which was discussed and planned out on a collect phone call from the private CCA Prison I was in before I was released. There were obstacles in the way due to the fact that upon my release I would have to return to Michigan to complete my parole since I had no immediate family members in Tennessee that I could parole home to. In order for us to make our plans come to fruition, we decided to go ahead and get married the day after I was released which was on March 1, 2002. This allowed me to parole home to my wife in Tennessee instead of having to return to Michigan to complete my 2 years parole.

It was a blessing to have my parole transferred to Tennessee. I felt like I was getting a fresh start at life and I had a strong circle of supporters around me to encourage and inspire me to make some great things happen. Our initial marriage took place in my Motherin-law and Father-in-law's living room. Pastor Adrian Simpson was present and ready to bring us both together in holy matrimony. Before we exchanged vows I had to sit down to have a man to man conversation with my Father-in-law. I asked him for his blessing to take his daughters hand in marriage. He mentioned to me that he and his wife had talked about me leading up to this special day and he remembered my Mother-in- law explaining to him that out of the few guys Chantelle had ever dated, I was the only one that she cried to her mother about when I left and returned to Detroit back in 1991.

My Father-in-law also known as Larry Patton Sr, explained to me with a straight poker face that he extends his blessing but he wanted to make sure he was clear that he didn't play about his children, but he would literally kill somebody about his grandchildren. I explained to him that I shared that same sentiment and assured him that I was going to protect his daughter and grandson with my life.

Pastor Simpson brought us together before God and helped us to become ONE as husband and wife. Several months later on June 8, 2002 we had one of the most amazing weddings on the planet. We had a beautiful traditional wedding at a church filled with people who loved and cared for us both.

I had the pleasure of having a lot of my family members travel from Detroit and Atlanta to witness my wife and I say I do. I had the honor of having two Best Men. Tom Adams was one of my Best Men and my brother William Berry Jr was my second Best Man. Jessica Taylor was also there to support me and my new wife Chantelle on our special day. Tom and Jessica's presence really meant a lot to us, but even more so to me. I came home to a very supportive circle of people. My mom, my sister and my entire family were there for me. My Mother-in-law, Father-in-law, Brother-in-law and all of my in-laws were there to support me as well.

My wife Chantelle and I initially met back in 1991 while I was living in Nashville Tennessee at the Kenmont Apartments with a few of my Job Corp brothers, Big Moe, Pops aka Demetris Robinson and Tyrone Lott. I met Chantelle and one of her best friends Deshawn Jordan at a Walgreens close by my apartments off of Dickerson Road.

I introduced myself to both of them while Chantelle was kneeling down searching a shelf for some paper for one of her college courses. She looked me up and down with a slight frown on her face as if I was getting on her nerves or smelled bad or something. I continued to pursue her anyway because I was definitely up for the challenge, plus she was so beautiful to me that

I couldn't let her get away without at least getting her phone number. She decided to take my phone number instead and waited almost a week before she called me. We dated for a few months before I decided to return home to Detroit because my roommate and I didn't have enough money to pay our rent and bills because of partying and not putting money up for rainy days like our trade school instructors suggested. We were in the masonry construction business which meant if it rained, we didn't work and if we didn't work, we didn't get paid. I have to admit that I was also homesick so I decided to pack it up and left without saying goodbye.

Who would've known that I would return, leave again in 1993, go to prison, serve 9 years, return again, get married and take on the role of being a husband and father figure to a beautiful wife and a wonderful stepson named Tez Corley? Tez was 8 years old when his mom and I got married and now he's 28 years old, he's an entrepreneur, he's very responsible, and he's living out his journey in his own place on the west coast. Us three moved to Texas on August 11th 2004. My wife and I have been married now for 19 years as of March 1, 2021.

It was unfortunate that Dymond Entertainment never took off like we expected it to, but I did however live out a portion of that dream by landing a job with my wife's best friend's brother's marketing and promotions company. I was given an opportunity to tour around the country putting on hip hop and R&B concerts while marketing products for partnering companies like BET, P&G, Coca Cola and the list goes on. I got a chance to hang out with some of the hottest hip hop and R&B artist in the game and had realized that I had once spoken these things out of my mouth while walking around the track on the prison yards back 40.

I worked on a variety of events including the Ebony Black Family Reunion Tour, The Totalemente Tour, The Pantene Total You Tour and the televised BET Black College Tour just to name a few. I served as an Operations Manager and Project Manager for Grassroots Promotions seasonally for approximately 7 ½ years. Touring usually lasted for approximately 9 months out of each year. Hopping from one tour to the next became second nature. This was a very exciting job for me considering I still had a desire to be involved in the music industry.

The time came when companies were cutting back because of the recession that hit America pretty hard back in 2008 and Grassroots Promotions was not getting the contracts signed to do tours like they had done so consistently in the past. Between working seasonal shows with Grassroots Promotions and constantly searching for work that paid a decent wage when I returned home after tours, I became really depressed at the fact that no one wanted to give me a chance earning a wage that I felt that I was worth. I was unable to provide for my family the way that I knew I needed to. No one would hire me it seemed, and if they did, it was because I had lied on my application hoping that they wouldn't find out at least until I got a few pay checks. It was really difficult for me to understand why people wouldn't give me a chance when I felt that I was more than qualified to do the job.

Regardless of how I felt, I knew that I needed to rely on my Lord and Savior Jesus Christ to get me through this difficult time. I decided to turn it all over to God and let Him fight the battle for me. It was in 2010 when my wife and I decided to sacrifice for a few months with no income coming in from me at all, which became a norm when the tours ended in mid-November of each year right after the BET Black College Tours.

I decided that I wanted to attend classes at a school that helped ex-felons learn a skill of operating CNC machines. I did my research to see what machine operator's annual income looked like and was pleased with what I found so I decided to go for it. The school I attended was called His Bridge Builders located in Dallas, TX. His Bridge Builders is a spiritually based program that relies on government funding and sponsors to help fund helpful programs to help men and women that want and need another chance at pursuing the American Dream.

I was introduced to a mentor by the name of Mark Lichty whom I would meet with periodically to pray, discuss the bible and just talk about life in general. We also went over plans to find the right job to fit the skills that I obtained through His Bridge Builders. It's only by the Grace of God this opportunity was made possible for me because of my wife's beautician and her husband's relationship with one of the Bridge Builders instructors. Charles Armelin was that instructor. He helped me get into the program and he also served as a mentor to each and every student in the class.

I successfully graduated from the program but still felt a little discouraged about trying to find a good job with a tainted background tagging along over my head like a black cloud. A very good friend of mine and brother in Christ by the name of

Michael Parker asked me to email him my resume so he could see if he could put it in the right hands. Not even a week later I received a call from the company that Mike worked at which was CFD International, also known as Contract Fabrication & Design. They called me on a Monday asking me to come in the next day to interview, but I needed to put it off until Wednesday instead. I almost couldn't believe it because I knew that Mike worked for a Private Defense Contractor building and designing weapon mounts for military helicopters. With a background like mine I knew that this was probably going to be a waste of my time and theirs.

The next day I attended a bible study at a local restaurant with some fellow Christian brothers that met once a week. This study was led by Evangelist Craig Nedro. These brothers prayed with me about getting the job at CFD, even though Craig Nedro kindly offered me a job at a local car dealership weeks before. Craig told me that I was hired if I wanted the job but allowed me time to see if the job at CFD would actually come through for me. A host of family and friends prayed with me with hopes that the good Lord would bless me with a job at CFD so that I could be able to provide for my family in a way that I hadn't been able to do over the years consistently since being home from prison.

So here it was, the day of my interview. I could hear my mentor Tom Adams in my head saying 'wear a suit.' Tom's pet peeve is seeing a man show up for an interview without a suit on. I decided to wear my 3 piece pinstripe suit. On my way there I called one of my good Christian friends named

Willandro Grant, who was also one of my tour roadies on the BET Black College Tour. Big Will, Cedric Lott and I used to pray every morning on our way to each HBCU event site throughout the USA. I called Big Will because I knew that he was active in his Dads church and I also knew that when 2 or more are gathered in his name God is in the midst.

I also listened to one of my favorite gospels songs by Yolanda Adams, 'In The Midst Of It All' which made me cry every time I listened to it. I finally arrived at my interview about 45 minutes early and saw the Production Managers that were going to interview me leaving for lunch. When they returned they were in awe and stated that they thought I was a customer or a government official based on the way that I was dressed and what I was driving. Before the interview began I could remember some advice given to me by another one of my mentors Brad Popoff telling me to give them the bad stuff first instead of giving it to them last which I believe helped me out tremendously.

I opened by saying " Before we begin, I'd like to mention that over 17 years ago I made some really bad decisions and those decisions sent me to prison to serve a 9 year sentence. I am not the same person that I was back then and have a paper trail of certificates and awards to prove how dedicated I am to staying on the right track. I've been a married man for 8 years, we have a son, and I'm also a homeowner with a house fully furnished, so I don't need to steal or take anything from anyone." They kept me in the interview for almost 2 hours. They were impressed and they showed me around the facility and I was amazed to see some of the equipment they used to do what they did. I actually started to fill like I had a chance at getting the job and was more than ready to do the second interview.

A couple of weeks had gone by since the

interview and I was beginning to get a little discouraged because they really seemed to like me on the interview, but I just couldn't get it out of my head that I was a convicted felon and convicted felons don't get jobs like that. I was starting to wonder if I should go ahead and take the car dealership job but something inside kept telling me to hold off and keep praying. Thank God for the positive circle of supporters that was in my corner during that difficult time.

After leaving multiple voicemails and driving my friend Mike up the wall asking had he heard anything, Mike called me and said that he spoke with the CEO Mr. Bill Gordon and asked him if he could at least give me the second interview. Mr. Gordon asked Mike, "Why should I hire someone with a criminal background when I could just hire anybody off the street without a background?" Mike explained to Mr. Gordon that I was a saved and dedicated servant in the church. He also mentioned the fact that I was married, we were home owners and I just needed someone to give me a second chance.

Mr. Gordon agreed to interview me himself, so they called me in for the interview a day after I had received the good news from Mike. At this point I knew that there was a strong possibility that I could actually convince them to hire me for the job despite my criminal record. I was a bit worried, but I knew if God willed it to come to pass, it would be. I called Willandro again to pray because it seemed like the first prayer with him worked. He prayed and I cried a good portion of the way there.

When I pulled into the parking lot my eyes were bloodshot red, but I was early enough to let them clear up before walking into the interview. Finally I walked into the interview with my head high and trying my best to look as sophisticated as possible. I wanted to impress Mr. Gordon and anyone else that I came in contact with. I interviewed with the CEO Mr. Bill Gordon, the Chief Engineer Mr. Russell Mensch and a host of other Department Heads at CFD for a little over 3 ½ hours. The interview went really well and God was definitely in the building. Mr. Gordon ended the interview with stating that he would speak with the Board of Directors and the owner of CFD Mrs. Betty Sanderson to see what they thought about hiring me in.

I was contacted the next day and told that I got the job! At that very moment I couldn't do nothing but say Thank You Jesus! I knew at that very moment that people who owned their own companies could do whatever they wanted to do regarding hiring people in with criminal backgrounds.

I was in complete awe knowing that I had just landed a job working for a Defense Contractor and there was NOTHING no one could tell me negative about the power of prayer because I had just been given a second chance. Mr. Gordon and Mrs. Sanderson still have my loyalty today if they ever call me and need my help for anything. They gave me an opportunity to work with

CFD for over 5 years before I got laid off. It was devastated when I lost my job, but as strangely as this may sound, I was also relieved.

Working for CFD was life changing for me and very helpful to my family. To be able to earn a decent wage for ANY man gives a boost to his self-esteem and self- confidence. They allowed me to become a part of their CFD family and had trusted me with projects that were really crucial, that if not done right the first time could cost missing deadlines and hundreds of thousands of dollars in losses. I started working for CFD as a contractor on July 12, 2011 and was hired in as a fulltime employee on my birthday November 5, 2011 which was also on a Saturday.

I was asked to come in for a few hours just to take some trash to the dump. My boss Mike Fellegy pulled me to the side that day and broke the good news to me that I was now a CFD employee and I was getting an immediate raise in pay. I was floored again at the miraculous favor that God had bestowed upon my life. Working at CFD was truly a blessing for not only me, but also the people that I've been able to help financially. The guys that I worked with became a part of my extended family. We pulled practical jokes on each other daily, we ate lunch together and we met up from time to time off the clock to participate in fantasy football drafts or just to challenge each other in a few games of pool.

I have to admit that during political season things would get really tense there because some of them couldn't stand President Barack Obama. A few of them would get really angry about the first black President which really made me start to feel a little uncomfortable since everybody was carrying weapons to work except for me.

I was hoping that no one would ever come in and snap in the workplace because they knew what my political beliefs were, not to mention me being a black man. I was happy that we had our first black President but I didn't rub it in their faces because that could turn into a really bad situation for me if someone came in unstable one day with a loaded pistol on their side.

Most of the people there were okay but periodically when someone new would start the job there I was a little concerned. There was one new employee that offered to help me load up some equipment being shipped out one night. He later went home and blew his brains out. That devastated us all! All I could think about is what if he had decided to do it while at work while helping me? With all of the racial tension going on around the world because of the hatred for a black

President, watching people's daily behavior at work also became a part of my personal job description.

I was actually pretty stressed some days going to work because the hate was pretty thick for President Obama. I ended up being the only black person working there after Mike left and Mr. Nelson began working at Mr. Gordon's aircraft hangar. I must say though, for the most part, I worked with some pretty great individuals at CFD that I still consider to be a part of my extended family even though we had different political views.

Working for CFD was truly a blessing.

11: RECOVERY

OCFD, things became quite stressful once I received my walking papers from considering the fact that my wife and I had just had our second home built and just closed on the loan a few months before. It was at that moment when I knew without a shadow of a doubt that I needed to pursue my dream of becoming a successful entrepreneur even more so!

I have to admit that even though I had just worked for a Defense Contractor around weapons that could tear an entire house down in a matter of seconds, I still felt inferior to everybody else when I picked up an application and came across that box that says, "Have you ever been convicted of a felony?" I had just worked for a company that sold military weapons and weapon mounts to the federal government and allies around the world but was denied getting a job driving a truck for a Soda Pop Company. This is when I knew for sure that I needed to quit playing games and start building my own business and brand!

My mom came up with a great idea years ago while I was serving time. While we were on a 15 minute collect call she mentioned to me that every time she searched for a greeting card to send me, she could never find the perfect card that suited my current situation. She had also noticed that every card I had sent her was custom made straight from the creative hands of some of my prison comrades. My mom knew that once I was released from prison it was gonna be difficult for me to get a good job with 3 felony convictions on my record, so she suggested that I create a greeting card business and specifically design them for people that are serving time in prisons all throughout the Country.

We both agreed that a greeting card sent to uplift men, women and children serving time in jails institutions and prisons could bring them hope, make them feel closer to their families and hopefully change the trajectory of their lives from bad to good. A card filled with words that would inspire them, reassure them that they are loved and words that, as my mom would say it, 'would tell it like it T.I. is!'

In the month of September 2013 I had already established the company Dymond Sentiments as an LLC. My big sister Carmen Berry blessed me with some of the money I needed to get everything established and to start bringing this great idea to fruition. I was able to establish the LLC and trademark my personal Dymond Logo. While in Virginia I had Bernard Platter create 4 different versions of the Dymond Logo because I knew that there were other things that I wanted to do in the Dymond name outside of music and entertainment.

There was one specific design that I wanted for myself because I wanted to use it for the greeting cards and clothing apparel. I shared the rest of those drawings with Greg because he had plans of opening up a custom auto paint shop as well. Greg and I told each other that no matter what happened between us as business partners, we were gonna be sure to establish businesses in the Dymond name. We were so dedicated to that vision that we even branded ourselves with Dymond tattoos.

While trying to figure out how to make this greeting card business work out successfully, I reflected on a powerful scripture in the Bible that I had followed to the best of my ability in the past. That scripture says, 'But seek ye first the kingdom of God, and His righteousness, and all these things shall be added unto you.'-Matthew 6:33. My wife and I attended our local church faithfully and we both served on a ministry.

After church hopping for a while, we decided we needed to find a church that was close to home because those one hour drives were beginning to take a toll on our cars and our gas tanks. When we finally found a church that we both were being fed at, I had begun the process of becoming a Deacon and my wife started to serve in the resource center. I had previously served as a Deacon at Community Christian Church in Nashville Tennessee under the leadership of Sr Pastor Adrian Simpson and his successor the late Sr Pastor Terry O Peaks right after returning home from prison.

Becoming a Deacon at The Potters House was quite different than my training in the past. There were several more requirements other than just attending a class and assisting with alter call, tithes, offering and communion. Before my actual Deacon training began I volunteered as a golf cart driver for one year transporting our visitors and congregation from their cars to the doors of the church every Sunday. I knew that I had to be consistent if I wanted the leaders of the Deacons ministry to know I was seriously ready to serve. After that year serving as a volunteer, I was added to the Deacon Ministry Class and was told that to become a Deacon with The Potters House I needed to commit to two years of training and I needed to be like liquid, which meant I needed to be flexible and ready to do and go wherever I was needed to serve.

There were a few times during that first year when I was wondering to myself, 'what have I gotten myself into' but each time I showed up, God revealed to me another reason why I set out on that journey. I thank Deacon Davila, Deacon Victor Rowe and the late Deacon Beacom for pursuing me as a candidate, even though I had planned on pursuing my place as a Deacon in The Potters House fold.

I expressed to Deacon Beacom that I had served time in prison and I wanted to get involved with the prison ministry. There was one time during my training that I didn't over communicate that my wife and I were going on vacation. Deacon Beacom called me while we were in Miami and said, "Hey man, I hadn't seen you and was wondering if you were still serious about becoming a Deacon." He was serious! I didn't take offense to it because he sounded like he really cared about my spiritual well-being.

I had communicated my travel plans to one of the leaders in the Deacon's ministry but I didn't mention it to him. This is when I learned it was better to over communicate so that everyone would be on the same page. One Sunday after church he took me back into the sanctuary after church had let out to meet Deacon Sephus and his wife Brenda Sephus. It was through this great dedicated couple that started me on my way into the prison ministry. After getting signed up, going through mandatory classes and getting a background check, I started going into a women's prison with our team of ministers with my wife right by my side.

I was a little nervous starting out and asked if I could observe for a while before throwing me out there. They honored my request the first few visits, but eventually called upon me to deliver a word from the Lord. One of our leaders of the prison ministry group contacted me one day and asked if I could volunteer to go into the Lew Sterrett County Jail with a brother by the name of Elder John Patton. Elder Patton and I were going in to the jails like the Dynamic Duo. Elder Ward teamed me up with a brother that I now love and respect like a big brother. My wife and I had also begun to go into another prison called Bridgeport Correctional Facility in Bridgeport Texas.

We traveled there every other Sunday with a variety of ministers from The Potters House main campus along with Deacon Sephus and his wife from the North campus. Pastor

Sheryl Brady and her husband Bishop Joby Brady resides over our congregation at the North Dallas Campus. Pastor Brady is a very powerful preacher and we are so very blessed to be a part of her and Bishop Joby Brady's flock. Before joining The Potter's House North Dallas my wife had mentioned to me that there was a Potter's House Church being held at the Dr. Pepper Arena in Frisco Texas.

I told my wife that I didn't want to attend a church that Bishop Jakes was not going to be there in person. I was under the impression that this church was a streaming church, but my wife said "no, this church has a Pastor named Sheryl Brady who was anointed and appointed to Pastor The Potter's House North Dallas. I have to admit that I was a little apprehensive about attending a church with a woman pastor, and to top it off, a white woman pastor. I did recall watching Joyce Meyer quite a bit in the past, but that was different because she was just a TV evangelist, or at least I thought. It wasn't like I was raised in the church, but what I thought I knew about church was that the Pastor was supposed to be a man.

Well one Sunday when my wife was under the weather with a cold, I decided to go and see what all the fuss was about with this white woman pastor that sounds like she's black when she's preaching. All I can say is that she preached to "ME" that day! The Deacons had opened arms for me in the narthex and when I went into the sanctuary the word of God was exactly what I needed to hear.

To myself, I was like, "this white woman can preach!" I returned home delighted to tell my wife that I believe we've found a church that's close to home and urged her to hurry up and get well so we could attend service that next following Sunday. That next Sunday she preached to both of us! We both looked at each other and said Wow! We knew at that very moment that we had found the church that we had been looking for, especially considering the fact that The Potter's House Dallas was too far to drive to because we love listening to Bishop Jakes. To see an entire family involved in ministry together with so much talent and a powerful anointing on their lives was all it took for us to wanna join the flock. Not to mention that Pastor Brady is from my hometown Detroit Michigan. My wife knew that if she told me Pastor Brady was from Detroit, I was really gonna be ready to listen. I'm Detroit Michigan everything!

I thank God daily for the journey He has allowed me to travel on throughout my life. While growing up in Detroit I was never encouraged to go to church by my parents. I knew that my Mom believed in God because she often talked about God or the name of Jesus in conversations, but we never really went to church together except for approximately 10 to 15 times total that I can recall. My Dad would read the Bible periodically, but I can't remember him ever mentioning God to me or going to church ever.

I was outside playing on Sunday mornings with the other kids that didn't go to church. My two Grandmothers would mention God to me all the time but

I can actually count on one hand how many times I've been to church with both of them. There has always been something inside me knowing that God existed, but I never truly got to know Him until I was locked up in prison away from all of the everyday distractions of life.

While spending time in the Wayne County jail for 8 months waiting for trial, I was sent to a cell block where all the guys there were having bible studies every day. This seemed weird to me but yet peaceful. I had been in the County jail a few times before but had never seen anything like this. During this time I was quite upset with God for allowing my friend Vicki to die like she did, so wanted nothing to do with God at that moment in my life. I was asked by one of the inmates did I wanna join them for bible study, but I said no!

That 'no' didn't last though because the next day they were at it again having bible study, all 11 inmates but me. One of the guys asked me did I want to join them and I firmly replied back with "No I'm good!" I also had my 'don't ask me again look on my face. I sat on the iron table in the middle of the prison floor and watched the television while these brothers were having discussions about people in the bible.

I started to hear the brothers sing gospel hymns which began to make me feel a way that I can't explain in words. I began pacing the floor back and forth passing the area where the brothers were having study and worship, but I couldn't find it in my heart to trust God again at that moment. Finally after becoming overwhelmed with emotion, I stopped and made eye contact with one of the brothers that seemed to be the spiritual leader of the bunch. He asked everyone to stop what they were doing for a moment while he gestured to me to come in and join the study.

I immediately said yeah I'll join with tears rolling down my face. I was hurting really bad inside for a few reasons. One was because Vicki had just passed away while visiting my hometown Detroit with me at my Mom's house. Another reason was because of the crime that I had committed that put me in jail. I felt so very remorseful for doing such a thing, this was not me. It was like I was wide awake living in a nightmare! I was hurting bad, but I knew that what I had just done not only devastated the person I had robbed, which was my Landlord, but I had also devastated my family and would probably never see my Dad again outside of prison because the doctors had given him about 6 months to 1 year to live.

At that very moment I needed those brothers. They seemed to have had a pretty good relationship with a forgiving God that I didn't know so well at the time. I was more than ready to get to know Him. During my stay there, I managed to read the entire New Testament but still didn't completely understand what I had just read. After being shipped off to prison I stopped going to church because it was rumored that guys that went to church in prison were tree jumpers (pedophiles) and snitches. I was really concerned about what people thought of me at the time which reminds me of the time that Peter denied Jesus 3 times before the rooster crowed.

It wasn't until I was shipped to Jarrett, VA because of the prison overcrowding in Michigan and my cellmate John

Stewart aka Big Stew's persistence with wanting me to go to church with him on one particular Sunday in 1999. Big Stew would ask me every Sunday to go to church with him but I would always answer him with a "No, I'm good!" Stew asked me on several occasions did I wanna go to church with him and I would always say no!

Stew would never ask me more than once before he left the cell heading to church, but there was one particular day that I told him no, but something inside me said if he asks me again I'm going. It was at that moment when I realized that my spirit and flesh were in a battle, but my spirit overtook my flesh on that day.

Stew asked me again and I couldn't respond back yes quickly enough!

When we walked into that church that night I felt the Holy Spirit fill me and drop me down to the floor. I felt like the prodigal son, like I made it home, I cried like a baby. The Ministry servants came and prayed over me. It was on that day when I accepted Jesus Christ as my Lord and Savior and from that day moving forward I didn't care who knew that I went to church. I began to see things happen in my life that I knew that no one but God could make happen. Even looking back throughout all of the chaos in my life I knew that God had to be watching over me. He had His hedge of protection wrapped all around me.

12: DYMOND LIFE

So you're planted, so here I am living in Texas, someone once told me to bloom where blooming in a place that I had never even imagined living until 2004. I can recall a time back in the mid 1990's while serving time at the Muskegon Correctional Facility in Muskegon Michigan watching a few broadcast of Bishop TD Jakes on television.

The peculiar thing about this was, when I watched him preach it wasn't actually on the standard channels offered by our television network provider. If you ever owned a small black and white KTV, the brand where when the knobs got stripped or broke off, you would have to use a fork, a pair of pliers or something to change those channels. You may also know that if you could somehow place that knob right in between two channels, you may be able to catch a signal from a cable station that you normally wouldn't be able to get.

In prison we used this method to catch entertainment videos that were not provided to us through our cable network provider. Inmates would usually try this method late nights on the weekend after lights out. We would sneak to watch uncut rap videos with hopes to see women shaking it up down and all around. Well, on one particular night I was searching to see something that would be pleasing to my flesh, but in turn, I found something that was pleasing to my spirit.

Bishop TD Jakes was preaching. This man's voice and the way he looked, baldhead and all, reminded me of my Dad who had just passed in 1994 due to Congestive Heart Failure. Bishops voice was powerful like a Lion the same as my Dad's.

Bishop Jakes and the Holy Spirit definitely had my attention that night. My Dad was a very strong man with a strong voice that would lay hands on anybody that would try him or mess with anything that he considered being his, with me and our family being at the top of the list.

My Dad had an Armadillo shell, but he had a loving, caring and helpful heart. The difference between Bishop Jakes and my Dad was Bishop Jakes would lay hands on you to lift you up, but my Dad would lay hands on you to beat you down. While watching Bishops broadcast, I had no idea at the time that seeds were being planted into my spirit and prepping me for the future that I would soon encounter.

Finally the day had arrived at the Higher Ground Convocation in Washington DC in June 2017. It was time for me to be ordained as a Deacon in the Church. This was an amazing accomplishment for me, considering the fact that some people had once wrote me off because of the wicked person that I had become. When my name was called to proceed up to the Altar I couldn't do anything but thank God continuously in my head.

After all of the Deacon's in training were called, the line shifted back to the right and I ended up directly in front of the man that once preached to me in a prison cell. That man was Bishop TD Jakes. I also noticed that we were lined up with the Cross that hung on the wall behind the pulpit.

The oil had been prepared and the anointed hands of several Bishops were ready to do what God directed them to do. Once the anointed hands were laid, it was at that very moment when I felt a heavy burden being lifted. There were so many emotions going on inside of me and figuratively speaking I was on cloud 9. It felt as if I had been running in a marathon race and finally I had crossed the finish line.

Bishop Jakes wrapped his arms around me as I began to sob and thank God. All I could think of at that very moment was I knew that I had just made my Dad in Heaven proud. I knew that the Angels in Heaven were dancing for joy and giving my Dad a high 5 for seeing my life make a 180 degree turn and transform from street thug, drug addict and 3rd degree convicted felon to Deacon Brent Jackson.

God had changed my name the same way that He did with Abraham and the Angel did with Jacob. I believe that everything is in divine order, and the Bible say's: And we know that God causes all things to work together for good to those who love God, to those who are called according to His purpose. –Romans 8:28

Today, I am the founder and owner of Dymond Sentiments LLC, which is a greeting card company specifically, designed to provide families of men, women and children serving time in jails, institutions and prisons a better purchase option of greeting cards that fit their loved ones current situations in mind.

Please let me be clear that my intentions with my greeting card company is not with hopes that the prisons stay full just so I can make a profit. But to help change lives and at the same time help me build generational wealth which will help me provide better options to my family, friends and loved ones. Also to prevent people that came up in environments like me from going out making bad decisions just for a quick financial gain that could land them in a state or federal prison or maybe even death. Dymond Sentiments has also begun to dabble into a variety of merchandise, from footwear and apparel to coffee mugs and back packs to help us build our brand.

The journey I took to get where I'm at today I believe was divinely ordained. God is using me today to give hope to those that may feel hopeless and to inspire those that just need a push start. The Bible teaches us that we should not grow weary of doing good, for in due season we will reap, if we do not give up. - Galatians 6:9. My mess has ultimately turned into my message and it lets those that I share it with know that no matter how many things I went through or how many times I felt like giving up, God was there with me to carry me through the trenches.

I never gave up seeking Him no matter how bad things got and as a result of that, God has showered me with plenty of His Favor, Mercy and Grace. Today without a doubt I know that if I seek ye first the Kingdom of God and all of His righteousness, all things will be added unto me. I am a living witness of the supernatural power of God and I am so very grateful that He loves us so much that He gave His only begotten Son, that whosoever believeth in Him should not perish, but have everlasting life.

BIO OF: BRENT JACKSON

"Receiving an encouraging letter from someone on the outside could make the difference between life and death (for an inmate)."

~ Brent Jackson

If there was ever a prime example of an incarcerated person being successfully rehabilitated, Brent Jackson is it! As evidenced by his present success, Brent demonstrates that no matter how dismal the circumstances are, a positive outcome can be achieved! A life can be turned around, and it is Brent's mission to help make this attainable for as many people as possible.

Born into what can be described as a crime school environment, Mr. Jackson's surroundings and circumstances led him to a life and lifestyle that he would not have chosen on his own. Growing up black and male in Detroit, MI, where drugs permeated through the streets, it had become commonplace to be lured into objectionable activities as a means of survival. Consequently, Brent morphed into someone he never meant to become. Experimenting with drug use, among other things, led to some bad decisions, including some criminal activity. This path led to 9 years of incarceration in the State of Michigan prison system.

Early in Brent's life, even in the midst of challenges he faced, there were always certain people placed in his life with angelic presence and positive influence. These people recognized gifts in Brent that he didn't even see himself, like the middle school counselor who encouraged him to become a part of the Glee Club! To his amazement, Brent enjoyed being involved in this group and it left an imprint that continues to influence him.

Positive seeds were sown into Brent's life by various people. Another that was pivotal, was a good friend in prison who persistently invited Brent to church. Finally, Brent acquiesced and attended a service. Brent got saved that day and never turned back. His passion for Christ continues to grow daily and the manifestation of God's presence in his life is undeniable.

Brent's life is a story that clearly exhibits the redemptive power of a loving God if you allow Him to work in your life. All too familiar is the pain of feeling the stigma associated with being an ex-convict. Brent has gotten the fearful and skeptical stares, the employment rejections, and all that comes with trying to thrive with a criminal history. Nonetheless, he has overcome those things.

Successful studies at H.I.S. Bridge Builders, El Centro Continuing Education, and Collin College prepared Brent to consistently maintain gainful employment. Brent has excelled on the job in various roles in Sales, Management and technical fields. Now Brent is flexing his entrepreneurial muscle with his most recent endeavor as Founder of

D.Y.M.O.N.D Sentiments. The Mission of D.Y.M.O.N.D Sentiments is: "To encourage strong connections between the incarcerated and those who care about them by providing inspirational greeting cards written with their situations in mind."

An ordained Deacon at the Potter's House Church in North Frisco Texas, pastored by Sheryl Brady and Bishop Joby Brady under the leadership of Bishop T. D. Jakes. A lifetime member of the Chance for Life Program in Detroit, MI, Brent gets great fulfillment out of mentoring and giving words of encouragement to anyone who needs positive energy.

Brent is happily married to the love of his life, Mrs. Chantelle Jackson. They have a son, Tez, whom they are very proud of. Brent is excited about the launch of D.Y.M.O.N.D Sentiments. This devoted family man enjoys playing Chess, riding jet skis, playing pool, watching sports and travelling to new places.

www.ingramcontent.com/pod-product-compliance
Lightning Source LLC
Chambersburg PA
CBHW051407290426
44108CB00015B/2186